Pop Biographies

TIMOTHÉE CHALAMET
DUNE'S LEADING MAN
by Elizabeth Andrews

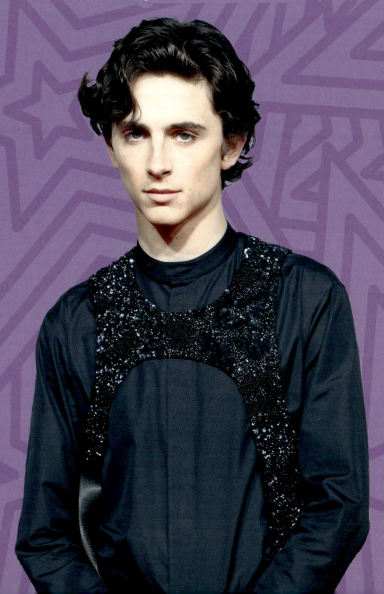

WELCOME TO DiscoverRoo!

This book is filled with videos, puzzles, games, and more! Scan the QR codes* while you read, or visit the website below to make this book pop.

popbooksonline.com/chalamet

abdobooks.com

Published by Pop!, a division of ABDO, PO Box 398166, Minneapolis, Minnesota 55419. Copyright © 2024 by Abdo Consulting Group, Inc. International copyrights reserved in all countries. No part of this book may be reproduced in any form without written permission from the publisher. DiscoverRoo™ is a trademark and logo of Pop!.

Printed in the United States of America, North Mankato, Minnesota.

052023
082023

THIS BOOK CONTAINS RECYCLED MATERIALS

Cover Photo: Getty Images

Interior Photos: Shutterstock Images, Getty Images, Sony Pictures Classics/courtesy Everett Collection, BFA/Alamy Stock Photo, PictureLux/The Hollywood Archive/Alamy Stock Photo

Editor: Grace Hansen
Series Designer: Colleen McLaren

Library of Congress Control Number: 2022950561

Publisher's Cataloging-in-Publication Data
Names: Andrews, Elizabeth, author.
Title: Timothée Chalamet: Dune's leading man / by Elizabeth Andrews
Other title: Dune's leading man
Description: Minneapolis, Minnesota : Pop!, 2024 | Series: Pop biographies | Includes online resources and index
Identifiers: ISBN 9781098244408 (lib. bdg.) | ISBN 9781098245108 (ebook)
Subjects: LCSH: Chalamet, Timothée--Juvenile literature. | Motion picture actors and actresses --Juvenile literature. | Planet Dune (Imaginary place)--Juvenile literature. | Actors--Juvenile literature.
Classification: DDC 782.42166092--dc23

*Scanning QR codes requires a web-enabled smart device with a QR code reader app and a camera.

TABLE OF CONTENTS

CHAPTER 1
Growing Up in NYC................ 4

CHAPTER 2
Breaking Out.................... 10

CHAPTER 3
The It Factor....................16

CHAPTER 4
Reaching Beyond the Stars...... 22

Making Connections............. 30
Glossary 31
Index........................... 32
Online Resources................ 32

CHAPTER 1
GROWING UP IN NYC

Timothée Hal Chalamet was born on December 27, 1995. He was raised in an apartment in New York City. Timothée and his sister were fourth-**generation** New Yorkers. His grandmother also lived in the same apartment building.

WATCH A VIDEO HERE!

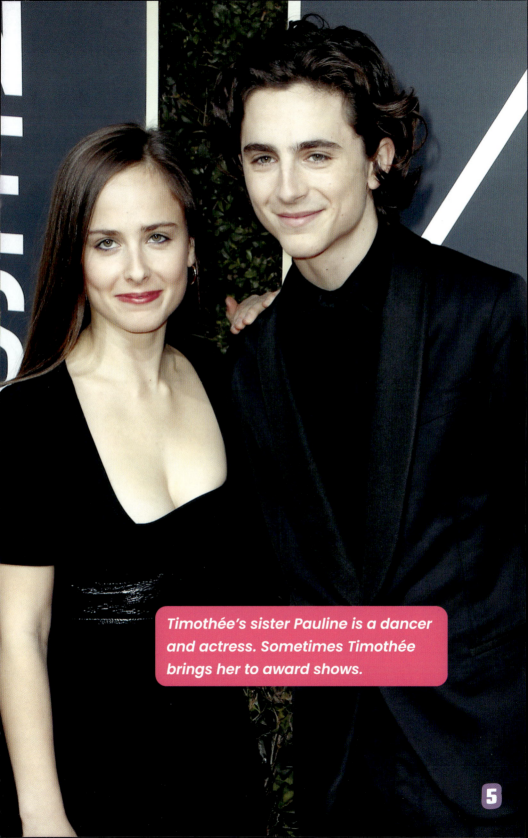

Timothée's sister Pauline is a dancer and actress. Sometimes Timothée brings her to award shows.

Timothée's father is French. He worked for an important worldwide children's charity. His mother was a Broadway dancer. Performing was in Timothée's blood. He says that he got his acting dreams from his mother and learned to be a good listener from his father.

Growing up, Timothée went to Fiorello H. LaGuardia High School of Music & Art and Performing Arts. The school is known

DID YOU KNOW? In high school, Timothée didn't get lead roles until his classmate, Ansel Elgort, graduated one year before him.

Timothée and Ansel were on a basketball team together.

for educating other famous stars like Nicki Minaj and Ansel Elgort. Timothée and his family spent summers in France. He speaks the French language very well.

Like many others, Timothée decided college was not the right path. Luckily there are many ways to find success as long as a person works hard.

While in school, Timothée played small roles in television shows and off-Broadway productions. After graduating in 2013, he gave college a try by attending NYU and Columbia University in New York City. But he realized he wanted to focus on acting and left after one year.

Like so many young people, Timothée's acting career didn't take off right away. But he wanted to take his time and wait for the right role. His first movies came out in 2014 and 2015. He played younger versions of Matthew McConaughey in *Interstellar* and James Franco in *The Adderall Diaries*.

Interstellar *is a movie about space explorers who work to protect humanity.*

CHAPTER 2
BREAKING OUT

While waiting for his first big opportunity, Timothée struggled with hearing the word "no" after trying out for roles. Sometimes he didn't even want to go see the movies he'd missed out on when they were released.

LEARN MORE HERE!

At the start of his acting career, Timothée struggled. He started to believe that he was dreaming too big.

The character Elio Perlman reads a lot in the film.

In 2016, Timothée was cast in his breakout role as Elio Perlman in *Call Me by Your Name*. The role was just right for Timothée. Elio was a 17-year-old boy who was spending the summer in Europe with his family. To play the part, Timothée had to learn Italian and learn to play the piano and guitar.

Call Me by Your Name came out in 2017 and got positive reviews. Timothée's performance was so impressive that he was **nominated** for Best Actor at the Academy Awards! Now the world knew who Timothée was and how great of an actor he could be.

Timothée became a regular on the red carpet in 2017.

DID YOU KNOW? The movies that made Timothée popular are called arthouse films. The films are high quality but are not made for huge audiences.

The year 2017 brought forth another hit movie called *Lady Bird*. It was written and **directed** by Greta Gerwig. Greta

Saoirse Ronan (right) *won best actress for her role in Lady Bird.*

could tell that Timothée would be a star. She also knew that he and costar Saoirse Ronan worked well together. The film, and Timothée's acting in it, once again impressed the public.

CHAPTER 3
THE IT FACTOR

After capturing the world's attention, Timothée starred in *Beautiful Boy* alongside Steve Carell in 2018. It was an emotional movie about a father and son going through a very hard time. For his part in *Beautiful Boy*, Timothée was **nominated** for several awards, including a Golden Globe for Best Supporting Actor.

EXPLORE LINKS HERE!

Kid Cudi is a rapper, songwriter, fashion designer, actor, and much more. He is one of Timothée's good friends. The two even lived together at one point.

The films that followed featured Timothée alongside superstars like Emma Watson, Selena Gomez, and Jude Law. Gerwig chose Timothée to play Laurie in the 2019 film *Little Women*. He would share the screen with Saoirse Ronan again. Fans of the classic novel by Louisa May Alcott were excited for the movie. The **ensemble** cast lived up to fans' expectations, and the movie won all kinds of awards!

DID YOU KNOW? The novel *Little Women* came out in 1868. The story follows the lives of four sisters.

The French Dispatch story is told as though it is a collection of magazine articles.

Following the success of *Little Women*, Timothée starred in *The French Dispatch*. This movie was written and **directed** by the famous Wes Anderson. Anderson is known for the **quirky** way he puts movies together. Timothée found it inspiring to work on a Wes Anderson film set.

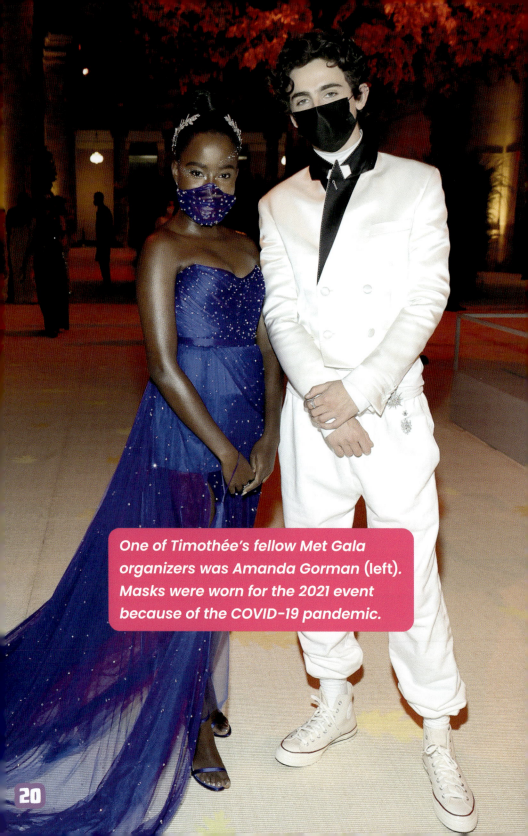

One of Timothée's fellow Met Gala organizers was Amanda Gorman (left). Masks were worn for the 2021 event because of the COVID-19 pandemic.

Timothée is known for playing deep and emotional characters. He once said of himself, "I feel like I'm here to show that to wear your heart on your sleeve is OK." Timothée earned the same level of recognition that the earlier **generation** of leading men got by playing tough action characters.

TIMMY AND FASHION

Along with acting, Timothée cares a lot about fashion. He is known to wear new and exciting things on red carpets. People like that he often wears clothes that are prettier and more delicate. In 2021, Timothée helped organize the Met Gala. It is considered a very important night in fashion. He famously mixed sweat pants with a tux jacket.

CHAPTER 4
REACHING BEYOND THE STARS

Timothée made a name for himself as an actor without being cast in a **blockbuster** movie. That's practically unheard of even for the most famous faces in Hollywood. Finally, Timothée landed the lead in the blockbuster

COMPLETE AN ACTIVITY HERE!

Before the big screen, Dune *was a series of books written by Frank Herbert.*

film *Dune*. The science fiction movie would cost $165 million and take three and a half years to make.

In the film, Timothée plays Paul Atreides, a man destined for greatness. The **director** of *Dune*, Denis Villeneuve, knew he wanted Timothée to play this role. Denis believed Timothée's smarts, **charisma**, and soulful eyes were perfect for the character.

Many called *Dune* a masterpiece. It picked up ten Oscar **nominations** including Best Motion Picture of the Year. Timothée was brought back to

DID YOU KNOW? Ever since director Denis Villeneuve read *Dune* as a teenager, he dreamed of making the book into a film.

continue Paul's story in *Dune: Part Two*. He was joined by even more famous cast members. Filming lasted from July to December 2022. The second installment was released in November 2023.

Timothée grew close with his Dune *costars Jason Momoa and Zendaya.*

OSCAR-NOMINATED FILMS

Interstellar

Call Me By Your Name

Lady Bird

Little Women

Dune

Don't Look Up

: Oscar winner

The Academy Awards are also called the Oscars. People work their whole lives to win an Oscar.

26

Between the two *Dune* films, Timothée starred in two other award-nominated films. In *Don't Look Up*, Timothée got to work with big stars like Leonardo DiCaprio and Jennifer Lawrence. In the romantic **horror** film *Bones and All*, Timothée teamed back up with the director of *Call Me by Your Name*.

Zendaya and Timothée's characters grow closer in the second Dune *movie.*

Timothée starred in Bones and All *with Taylor Russell (left). He wore accessories that looked like bones to red carpet events promoting the movie.*

Timothée likes to focus on having a positive impact on the world. He uses his platform to promote mental health care.

He also spends his time learning about **climate change**. He wears and supports fashion brands that care about the environment.

Timothée Chalamet is already a wildly successful actor. With new blockbusters lined up, his future is sure to be bright.

Timothée went by Timmy during his school years. But when he started acting, he wanted to use his full name.

MAKING CONNECTIONS

TEXT-TO-SELF

Timothée Chalamet struggled with disappointment when he didn't book roles at the beginning of his acting career. Can you think of a time in your life when you dealt with disappointment? How did you get through it?

TEXT-TO-TEXT

Have you read any other books about an actor? If so, how was that actor similar to or different from Timothée?

TEXT-TO-WORLD

Timothée cares about the environment. He wears clothes that are environmentally friendly. What are other ways people around the world try to care for the Earth?

GLOSSARY

blockbuster — a movie that is very large and successful.

charisma — a way of being that draws other people to you and makes them want to be around you.

climate change — a long-term change in Earth's climate, or in that of a region of Earth. It includes changing temperatures, weather patterns, and more.

direct — to carry out the organizing, energizing, and supervising of a film, play, or TV show. A person who directs is a director.

ensemble — a group of people who work or perform together. Usually the group is full of well-known people.

generation — all the people of about the same age within a society or within a particular family.

horror — a play, movie, or television show that frightens or scares the audience.

nominate — to choose as a possible winner for an award.

quirky — unusual in a positive way.

INDEX

Adderall Diaries, The, 9
awards, 13, 16, 18, 24, 26–27

Beautiful Boy, 16
Bones and All, 27

Call Me by Your Name, 12–13, 26–27

Don't Look Up, 26–27
Dune films, 23–26

family, 4, 6–7
fashion, 21, 29

French Dispatch, The, 19

Interstellar, 9, 26

Lady Bird, 14, 26
Little Women, 18–19, 26

New York City, NY, 4, 7–8

school, 6–8

This book is filled with videos, puzzles, games, and more! Scan the QR codes* while you read, or visit the website below to make this book pop.

popbooksonline.com/chalamet

*Scanning QR codes requires a web-enabled smart device with a QR code reader app and a camera.